THE KARMA'S SIGNATURE

THE COSMIC JUSTICE!

RAMYA SURESH SHAIVA

"Dedicated to my loving husband, Suresh Shaiva, and to all spiritual leaders, including Lord Buddha and the Supreme God Cosmos, who have guided me towards a greater understanding of the universal laws of karma. May this book serve as a testament to the transformative power of wisdom, compassion, and positive action in shaping our lives and the world around us."

With Gratitude !

Contents

Foreword   *vii*

Preface   *ix*

Acknowledgements   *xi*

Prologue   *xiii*

1. The Karma's Signature   1

Karma's Concept

2. The Science Of Karma   5

The Cause And Effect Of Karma

The Power Of Intention In Shaping Karma

The Impact Of Thoughts, Words, And Actions On Karma

3. Karma In Spiritual Practices   13

The Connection Between Karma And Rebirth

The Role Of Karma In Spiritual Evolution

The Relationship Between Karma And Enlightenment

The Practice Of Karma Yoga

4. Understanding Negative Karma   27

Recognizing The Causes Of Negative Karma

Overcoming The Effects Of Negative Karma

Transforming Negative Karma

The Role Of Self-reflection In Reducing Negative Karma

5. Practicing Positive Karma   37

The Benefits Of Positive Karma

The Cultivation Of Positive Thoughts,

Practicing Generosity, Compassion, And Kindness

Engaging In Selfless Acts For The Greater Good

6. Karma In Relationships   47

Contents

Building Positive Karma In Relationships

The Role Of Forgiveness And Understanding In Transforming Karma

    7. Karma And The Environment   53

The Benefits Of Creating Positive Karma For The Environment

    8. Karma And The Environment   57

Understanding The Challenges Of Karma

Overcoming Obstacles To Positive Karma

The Benefits Of Overcoming Challenges To Positive Karma

    9. Karma's Life 21 Tips   65

    10. Conclusion   69

The Impact Of Karma On Personal Growth And Happiness

Our Memories   75

Our Healing Classes   77

Our Energy Healing Classes   79

Our Energy Healing Classes   81

Our Memories   83

Our Feathers   85

How To Reach Us   87

Our Other Books   89

Free 30 Mins Counselling Session   91

Foreword

"The concept of karma has been a guiding principle for generations, shaping our beliefs and actions in profound ways. This book, 'Karma's Signature', offers a comprehensive and insightful examination of the principles of cause and effect and how they influence every aspect of our lives. From exploring the roots of karma in ancient wisdom traditions to providing practical guidance for how to live a virtuous life, this book is a must-read for anyone seeking to deepen their understanding of the universe and their place within it. So, let us embark on this journey together, discovering the ways in which we can cultivate positive karma and create a brighter future for ourselves and the world."

Preface

"The idea that our actions have consequences, both in this life and beyond, has captivated the human imagination for millennia. This preface introduces the reader to the book 'Karma's Signature', which provides a comprehensive and in-depth exploration of the concept of karma and its role in shaping our lives and the world around us. Through this book, we will examine the rich history and cultural diversity of the concept of karma, as well as its practical applications and how it can inform our daily actions. Whether you are a seasoned practitioner of karma or just beginning your journey of discovery, this book offers something for everyone. So, let us delve into the timeless wisdom of karma and learn how to live a life filled with purpose, joy, and positive impact."

Acknowledgements

"The journey of writing this book 'Karma's Signature' has been a rewarding and enlightening experience, and it would not have been possible without the support and inspiration of many individuals. I would like to express my gratitude to all those who have supported me along the way.

First and foremost, I would like to thank my beloved husband Sri.Suresh Shaiva and my family, who have always encouraged me in my pursuits and provided unwavering support during the writing process. I would also like to acknowledge the countless spiritual leaders and scholars, who have dedicated their lives to the study and teachings of karma, providing invaluable insight and wisdom that has informed this book.

I am also deeply grateful to my editors and reviewers, who have offered constructive feedback and helped to refine and shape the book.

Finally, I would like to extend my heartfelt thanks to all of you, the readers, who have shown interest in this book and are embarking on this journey of discovery with me. I hope that this book provides you with a deeper understanding of the workings of karma and the impact of our actions on the world.

With gratitude, Ramya Suresh Shaiva."

Prologue

"From the earliest moments of human history, the idea that our actions have consequences has captivated the imagination. The concept of karma, with its roots in ancient wisdom traditions, has provided a framework for understanding the intricate web of cause and effect that shapes our lives and the world around us.

In this book, 'Karma's Signature', we will explore the many facets of karma, from its history and cultural diversity to its practical applications in our daily lives. Whether you are a seasoned practitioner or just beginning your journey of discovery, this book offers a comprehensive understanding of the principles of karma and how they can inform and inspire us.

As you read, you will learn about the beliefs and practices surrounding karma in different cultures and religions, and how they have shaped our understanding of the universe and our place within it. You will also discover practical steps for how to live a virtuous life and create positive karma, and how to navigate the challenges and obstacles that life presents.

So, let us begin this journey of discovery together, exploring the timeless wisdom of karma and learning how to live a life of purpose, compassion, and positive impact. The story of karma is waiting to be written, and it begins now."

CHAPTER ONE

The Karma's Signature

The cosmic Justice System!

Understanding the concept of Karma is important for several reasons.

First, it helps us to take responsibility for our actions and thoughts. When we understand that our actions have consequences, we are more likely to be mindful of the impact we have on others and on the world around us. This understanding encourages us to make choices that are in line with our values and to act with kindness and compassion towards others.

Second, Karma provides a framework for personal growth and self-improvement. When we understand that our actions have consequences, we can use this knowledge to reflect on our behavior and make changes that will help us to grow and evolve. This can lead to a deeper sense of fulfillment and purpose in life.

Third, the concept of Karma helps us to understand the interconnectedness of all things. It reminds us that our actions and thoughts have a direct impact on the world and that we are all connected. This understanding can lead to a sense of compassion and empathy for others and can help us to create a more harmonious and peaceful world.

Finally, understanding Karma can help us to find peace and contentment in life. When we understand that our experiences are a result of our past actions and that we have the power to shape our future experiences through our current actions and thoughts, we can find a sense of control and stability in an otherwise uncertain world.

understanding the concept of Karma can have a profound impact on our lives. It can help us to take responsibility for our actions, encourage personal growth, deepen our understanding of the world, and bring peace and contentment to our lives.

Karma's concept

Karma is a concept in Hinduism, Buddhism, and Jainism that refers to the moral law of cause and effect. It is believed that every action, whether good or bad, has a corresponding effect that will determine a person's future experiences, circumstances, and destiny. The idea of Karma suggests that individuals are responsible for their actions and that their actions will shape their future experiences in this life and in future lives. This creates a cycle of cause and effect that can lead to spiritual growth and liberation or suffering and rebirth, depending on the nature of a person's actions.

Historical and cultural roots of Karma

The concept of Karma has roots in ancient Indian culture and philosophy. It is thought to have originated in the Vedic scriptures of Hinduism and was later incorporated into Buddhist and Jain traditions.

In Hinduism, Karma is mentioned in the Upanishads, which are ancient philosophical texts that explore the nature of the self, reality, and the ultimate truth. The concept of Karma was also developed by early Hindu thinkers such as the sage Patanjali, who wrote the Yoga Sutras.

In Buddhism, the idea of Karma was adopted and expanded upon as part of the Buddhist doctrine of rebirth. According to Buddhist teachings, a person's Karma is responsible for their rebirth in different realms of existence, such as the human realm, the celestial realm, or the hell realms.

The Jain tradition also recognizes the importance of Karma and believes that it is a crucial component of the path to liberation. In Jainism, it is believed that every action has a lasting impact on a person's soul and that by following the principles of non-violence, truthfulness, and non-stealing, one can accumulate positive Karma and progress towards liberation.

Overall, the historical and cultural roots of Karma can be traced back to ancient India, where it was developed as a central principle in various philosophical and spiritual traditions.

CHAPTER TWO

The Science of Karma

The concept of Karma is illustrated in many Hindu scriptures and myths, including the epic "Mahabharata." In this ancient Indian text, Karma is depicted as a powerful force that governs the lives of individuals and shapes their experiences.

One example from the ***"Mahabharata"*** that demonstrates how Karma works is the story of King Duryodhana. Duryodhana was a prince who was known for his cruelty and unjust actions, including the theft of his cousins' kingdom and the attempted murder of the Pandavas, his cousins. Throughout the story, Duryodhana is punished for his negative Karma, as his actions lead to conflict and violence, ultimately resulting in his defeat and death.

In contrast, the Pandavas, who are portrayed as virtuous and just, are rewarded for their positive Karma. Despite facing many challenges and obstacles, the Pandavas ultimately victory and are able to reclaim their kingdom, thanks to their good deeds and virtuous actions.

This example from the "Mahabharata" demonstrates how Karma works by showing that every action, whether positive or negative, has a corresponding effect that will determine an individual's future experiences. The story illustrates how a person's actions can shape their destiny and how negative actions can lead to future suffering, while positive actions can lead to future rewards.

Overall, the "Mahabharata" serves as a powerful example of how Karma works in Hinduism, demonstrating the idea that individuals are responsible for their actions and that their actions will shape their future experiences and destiny.

In real life, Karma can be seen in the way that people's actions come back to them, either in positive or negative ways.

For example, consider a person who is consistently kind and generous to others. They may find that good things come back to them, such as new friends, help when they need it, or opportunities to advance in their career. On the other hand, someone who is consistently selfish and cruel to others may find that their behavior comes back to haunt them, causing them to experience negative consequences such as loss of friends, difficulty in their career, or even legal trouble.

In this way, Karma can be seen as a kind of cosmic justice system, where good actions are rewarded and bad actions are punished. It's a reminder that our actions have real consequences, and that we should strive to act in ways that are kind and beneficial to others.

The cause and effect of Karma

The cause and effect of Karma is based on the idea that every action, thought, and intention we have creates energy that resonates in the universe. This energy, in turn, affects our future experiences and shapes our destiny.

In simple terms, the cause of Karma is our thoughts, words, and actions. The effect of Karma is the experiences, events, and circumstances that we encounter in our lives as a result of those actions.

For example, if we perform acts of kindness and generosity, the positive energy that we create through those actions will attract positive experiences and people into our lives. On the other hand, if we engage in harmful or negative behavior, the negative energy that we create will attract negative experiences and circumstances.

In this sense, Karma can be seen as a self-regulating system, where our actions have consequences that affect our future, encouraging us to make choices that promote positivity and well-being for ourselves and others.

The concept of karma is central to Hindu philosophy, including the Ramayana. According to this belief, the actions of an individual in this life determine their future in the next life, or rebirth. This is often referred to as the law of cause and effect, or ***"what goes around, comes around."***

In the Ramayana, the idea of karma is shown through the actions and consequences of various characters. For example, Ravana's evil deeds and mistreatment of Sita leads to his eventual downfall, while Rama's righteousness and obedience to dharma result in his eventual triumph. This reinforces the belief that good deeds will be rewarded, and evil deeds will lead to suffering.

In this way, the Ramayana demonstrates how karma shapes the lives of its characters and how it ultimately determines their destiny.

The power of intention in shaping Karma

The power of intention plays a crucial role in shaping one's karma. In many Eastern philosophical traditions, it is believed that thoughts, words, and actions all contribute to the creation of karma. Intentions serve as the driving force behind our actions, and it is the quality of these intentions that determine the impact they have on our karma.

When we act with positive intention, our actions are more likely to produce positive results. On the other hand, when our intentions are negative, our actions may cause harm to ourselves and others, leading to negative consequences in the future. It's important to note that our intentions aren't always conscious; sometimes we act out of habit, fear, or ignorance, which can also influence the quality of our karma.

One way to cultivate positive intentions is through mindfulness. By paying attention to our thoughts and motivations, we can become aware of our intentions and work to redirect them in a positive direction. Additionally, practices like meditation, self-reflection, and acts of kindness can help us cultivate a more positive mindset, which can lead to more positive actions and ultimately better karma.

the power of intention plays a crucial role in shaping our karma. By cultivating positive intentions through mindfulness and positive practices, we can improve the quality of our karma and create a more positive future for ourselves and others.

The impact of thoughts, words, and actions on Karma

The impact of thoughts, words, and actions on Karma is a central concept in Eastern philosophical traditions, including Hinduism and Buddhism. This belief holds that everything we think, say, and do influences our karma and shapes our future experiences.

One example from Hindu mythology that illustrates this concept is found in the Mahabharata. In this epic, the warrior prince Yudhishthira is advised by the sage Bhishma that his **thoughts, words, and actions are all seeds that will bear fruit in the future**. Bhishma likens the creation of karma to the planting of seeds in a field, explaining that just as the seeds a farmer plants will determine the crops he will reap, the thoughts, words, and actions we plant in the present will determine the experiences we will have in the future.

An analogy that is often used to explain the impact of thoughts, words, and actions on karma is that of a ripple in a pond. Just as a single stone thrown into a pond creates ripples that spread outwards, our thoughts, words, and actions also have a ripple effect, influencing the lives of those around us and the world in general. The bigger the stone, or the more positive the intention behind our thoughts, words, and actions, the greater the positive impact we can have.

the belief in the impact of thoughts, words, and actions on karma is central to Eastern philosophical traditions and is represented in Hindu mythology through the example of Yudhishthira in the Mahabharata, as well as through the analogy of a ripple in a pond. By cultivating positive thoughts, words, and actions, we can create

positive karma and ultimately shape a better future for ourselves
and those around us.

CHAPTER THREE

Karma in Spiritual Practices

Karma plays a significant role in many spiritual practices, including meditation, mindfulness, and acts of selflessness or compassion. These practices can help us cultivate positive karma and create a more positive future for ourselves and others.

Meditation, for example, can help us develop self-awareness and understand the motivations behind our thoughts, words, and actions. By observing our mind and becoming aware of our tendencies, we can redirect our thoughts and actions in a positive direction and create positive karma.

Mindfulness, which involves paying attention to the present moment, can also help us cultivate positive karma. When we are mindful, we are more likely to act with intention and make conscious choices that align with our values. This can lead to more positive experiences in the present and better karma in the future.

Acts of selflessness and compassion, such as volunteering, donating to charity, or helping someone in need, can also help us create positive karma. By putting the needs of others before our own and acting with kindness, we can generate positive energy and cultivate positive intentions.

spiritual practices such as meditation, mindfulness, and acts of selflessness and compassion can play an important role in shaping our karma. By incorporating these practices into our lives, we can cultivate positive intentions, make conscious choices, and ultimately create a more positive future for ourselves and others.

The connection between Karma and rebirth

The connection between Karma and rebirth is a central belief in many Eastern philosophical traditions, including Hinduism. This belief holds that the actions and intentions of an individual in one lifetime will determine their experiences in future lives through the cycle of rebirth.

One example from Hindu mythology that illustrates this connection is found in the Ramayana. In this epic, the prince Rama is depicted as being born into a life of privilege and destined for greatness. However, through his thoughts, words, and actions, he cultivates positive karma and eventually becomes the embodiment of virtue and goodness. This positive karma ensures that he will be reborn into a life of even greater privilege and success in the future.

The connection between Karma and rebirth is often described as cause and effect. Just as our actions and intentions in the present can determine our experiences in the future, our experiences in past lives are said to have been shaped by our actions and intentions in those lives. This cycle of rebirth continues until an individual has purified their karma and achieved liberation from the cycle of birth and death.

An analogy that is often used to explain the connection between Karma and rebirth is that of a farmer planting seeds. Just as the farmer chooses the seeds he plants and the soil he plants them in, our thoughts, words, and actions in this life determine the experiences we will have in future lives. By planting positive seeds, we can ensure a better harvest in the future.

the connection between Karma and rebirth is a central belief in many Eastern philosophical traditions and is illustrated in Hindu mythology through the example of Rama in the Ramayana. By cultivating positive thoughts, words, and actions in this life, we can create positive karma and shape a better future for ourselves in future lives through the cycle of rebirth.

The role of Karma in spiritual evolution

The role of Karma in spiritual evolution is a belief that holds that our experiences in life, both positive and negative, serve to help us grow and develop as spiritual beings. This growth is achieved through the accumulation of positive karma and the resolution of negative karma, which is said to occur over multiple lifetimes.

One real-life example that illustrates the role of Karma in spiritual evolution is the story of Nelson Mandela. Mandela, who was a former president of South Africa and a political prisoner for 27 years, is widely regarded as one of the great spiritual leaders of the 20th century. Through his thoughts, words, and actions, he cultivated positive karma by dedicating his life to the service of others and working towards the betterment of his country and its people. Despite facing enormous obstacles and adversity, Mandela never lost sight of his values and remained steadfast in his commitment to justice and equality.

Through his experiences, Mandela demonstrated the transformative power of positive karma and the role it can play in spiritual evolution. By choosing to act with kindness, compassion, and selflessness, Mandela was able to create positive energy and bring about positive change in the world. In this way, his experiences helped him to evolve as a spiritual being and inspired others to do the same.

Another example that illustrates the role of Karma in spiritual evolution is the story of the Tibetan monk and Nobel Peace Prize laureate, the Dalai Lama. Despite facing years of exile and persecution, the Dalai Lama has remained steadfast in his commitment to compassion, non-violence, and the pursuit of peace. Through his actions and his tireless work to promote human rights and dignity, the Dalai Lama has cultivated positive karma and become a beacon of hope and inspiration for people all over the world.

the role of Karma in spiritual evolution is an important belief in many spiritual traditions. Through our thoughts, words, and actions, we can cultivate positive karma and use our experiences in life to help us grow and evolve as spiritual beings. Real-life examples, such as the stories of Nelson Mandela and the Dalai Lama, demonstrate the transformative power of positive karma and the role it can play in spiritual evolution.

The relationship between Karma and enlightenment

The relationship between Karma and enlightenment is a central belief in many spiritual traditions, including Hinduism and Buddhism. This belief holds that our actions in this life, both positive and negative, shape our experiences and determine our path towards spiritual awakening.

In the context of the Isha Foundation, founded by Sadhguru, enlightenment is seen as the ultimate goal of human existence. Sadhguru emphasizes the importance of positive karma in the journey towards enlightenment, as it helps to purify the mind and prepare the individual for a deeper spiritual experience. By engaging in selfless service, practicing compassion and non-violence, and cultivating positive thoughts, words, and actions, individuals can create positive karma and move closer to enlightenment.

Sadhguru also stresses the importance of resolving negative karma from past lives, which can block individuals from achieving spiritual progress. He teaches that this can be achieved through a variety of practices, such as meditation and yoga, which help to purify the mind and resolve negative energy. By resolving negative karma, individuals can free themselves from the cycle of birth and death and move closer to enlightenment.

the relationship between Karma and enlightenment is a central belief in many spiritual traditions. According to Sadhguru and the Isha Foundation, the accumulation of positive karma and the resolution of negative karma play an important role in the journey towards enlightenment. By cultivating positive thoughts, words, and actions, and resolving negative karma through practices such as meditation and yoga, individuals can move closer to spiritual awakening and experience a greater sense of inner peace and fulfillment.

The relationship between Karma and enlightenment is also a central belief in the teachings of Sri Sri Ravi Shankar and the Art of Living Foundation. Like Sadhguru and the Isha Foundation, Sri Sri Ravi Shankar emphasizes the importance of positive karma in the journey towards enlightenment. He teaches that individuals can create positive karma by engaging in selfless service, practicing compassion and non-violence, and cultivating positive thoughts, words, and actions.

In the Art of Living tradition, enlightenment is seen as a state of inner peace and bliss, where the mind is free from all thoughts and negative emotions. Sri Sri Ravi Shankar emphasizes that this state can be achieved by purifying the mind and resolving negative karma from past lives. He teaches that this can be done through practices such as meditation and yoga, as well as through acts of kindness, compassion, and selflessness.

Another example of the relationship between Karma and enlightenment in the teachings of Sri Sri Ravi Shankar is the practice of Karma Yoga. Karma Yoga is a form of yoga that emphasizes the importance of action and service in the journey towards enlightenment. By engaging in selfless service and working towards the betterment of others, individuals can create positive karma and move closer to enlightenment.

the relationship between Karma and enlightenment is a central belief in the teachings of Sri Sri Ravi Shankar and the Art of Living Foundation. Like Sadhguru and the Isha Foundation, Sri Sri Ravi Shankar emphasizes the importance of positive karma and the resolution of negative karma in the journey towards spiritual awakening. Through practices such as meditation, yoga, and selfless service, individuals can purify the mind, create positive karma, and move closer to enlightenment.

Sadhguru and Sri Sri Ravi Shankar both have a similar approach to the relationship between Karma and enlightenment. They both believe that the accumulation of positive karma and the resolution of negative karma play a crucial role in the journey towards spiritual awakening. Both emphasize the importance of positive thoughts, words, and actions, as well as the resolution of negative karma through practices such as meditation, yoga, and selfless service.

Both Sadhguru and Sri Sri Ravi Shankar also stress the importance of living a life of compassion, kindness, and non-violence. They believe that by practicing these values, individuals can create positive karma and move closer to enlightenment. They both view enlightenment as a state of inner peace and bliss, where the mind is free from negative thoughts and emotions.

In terms of teaching methods, both Sadhguru and Sri Sri Ravi Shankar are known for their engaging and accessible teaching styles. They both use anecdotes, humor, and everyday examples to convey complex spiritual concepts in a way that is easy to understand. Both are also respected spiritual leaders, who have inspired millions of people around the world with their teachings.

Sadhguru and Sri Sri Ravi Shankar have a similar approach to the relationship between Karma and enlightenment. Both view the accumulation of positive karma and the resolution of negative karma as crucial in the journey towards spiritual awakening, and both emphasize the importance of compassion, kindness, and non-violence in creating positive karma. Both are also known for

their engaging and accessible teaching styles, and are respected
spiritual leaders who have inspired many people around the
world.

The practice of Karma yoga

Karma Yoga is a central concept in the Bhagavad Gita, an ancient Hindu scripture. In the Bhagavad Gita, Lord Krishna explains to Prince Arjuna that Karma Yoga is the path of action and selfless service. It involves performing actions without attachment to the results or fruits of those actions. This means that individuals should perform their duties and responsibilities without becoming attached to the outcomes, and without expecting anything in return.

Karma Yoga is seen as a way to purify the mind and resolve negative karma from past lives. By performing actions without attachment, individuals can cultivate a state of inner peace and contentment, and move closer to enlightenment. The Bhagavad Gita teaches that Karma Yoga is a key part of the spiritual journey, and that individuals who practice it will experience greater happiness, inner peace, and fulfillment in life.

An analogy for Karma Yoga might be a gardener who tends to a garden without any attachment to the outcome. The gardener simply performs their duties, caring for the plants and maintaining the garden, without expecting anything in return. They do so simply because it is their duty and they enjoy doing it. In the same way, an individual practicing Karma Yoga performs their actions and duties without attachment to the outcome, and simply because it is their duty and they find fulfillment in doing so.

Karma Yoga is a central concept in the Bhagavad Gita, and is seen as a path of action and selfless service. By performing actions without attachment, individuals can purify the mind and resolve negative karma, and move closer to enlightenment. The practice of Karma Yoga can bring greater happiness, inner peace, and fulfillment in life, and is an important part of the spiritual journey.

A real-life example of Karma Yoga can be seen in the work of Mother Teresa. Mother Teresa was a Catholic nun who dedicated her life to serving the poor and sick in the slums of Kolkata, India. Despite the difficult conditions and limited resources, Mother Teresa performed her duties with love, compassion, and selfless service. She did so without attachment to the outcome or expectation of recognition or reward.

Mother Teresa's work was a manifestation of Karma Yoga in action. She performed her duties without any expectations, simply because it was her duty to serve and help others. She found fulfillment and happiness in serving others, and her actions had a profound impact on the lives of the people she helped.

Another real-life example of Karma Yoga is the work of volunteers and aid workers in disaster-stricken areas. These individuals often work long hours in difficult conditions, providing essential aid and support to those in need. They do so without any expectation of recognition or reward, and simply because it is their duty to help those in need.

The real-life examples of Karma Yoga can be seen in the work of individuals who perform their duties and responsibilities with love, compassion, and selfless service. These individuals, like Mother Teresa and aid workers, perform their actions without attachment to the outcome and simply because it is their duty to help others. Their actions demonstrate the power of Karma Yoga in bringing about positive change in the world and helping individuals move closer to enlightenment.

Negative karma is a term used to describe the negative consequences that can result from negative thoughts, words, and actions. According to the concept of karma, individuals are responsible for the consequences of their own actions. When individuals engage in negative thoughts, words, and actions, they create negative karma, which can result in negative consequences in their lives.

Examples of negative thoughts, words, and actions include anger, hatred, jealousy, greed, and dishonesty. These negative actions can cause harm to others and create negative energy that can linger in the individual's mind and environment. Over time, this negative energy can manifest as negative consequences, such as illness, poverty, relationship problems, and other challenges.

It is important to note that negative karma can be resolved through positive thoughts, words, and actions. By engaging in positive behaviors, individuals can create positive karma, which can help to counteract the effects of negative karma. For example, practicing kindness, compassion, and selfless service can help to resolve negative karma and bring positive consequences into an individual's life.

negative karma is a concept that describes the negative consequences that can result from negative thoughts, words, and actions. Negative karma can be resolved through positive thoughts, words, and actions, and can be a powerful motivator for individuals to live a more positive and virtuous life.

CHAPTER FOUR

Understanding Negative Karma

Negative karma is a term used to describe the negative consequences that can result from negative thoughts, words, and actions. According to the concept of karma, individuals are responsible for the consequences of their own actions. When individuals engage in negative thoughts, words, and actions, they create negative karma, which can result in negative consequences in their lives.

Examples of negative thoughts, words, and actions include anger, hatred, jealousy, greed, and dishonesty. These negative actions can cause harm to others and create negative energy that can linger in the individual's mind and environment. Over time, this negative energy can manifest as negative consequences, such as illness, poverty, relationship problems, and other challenges.

It is important to note that negative karma can be resolved through positive thoughts, words, and actions. By engaging in positive behaviors, individuals can create positive karma, which can help to counteract the effects of negative karma. For example, practicing kindness, compassion, and selfless service can help to resolve negative karma and bring positive consequences into an individual's life.

The negative karma is a concept that describes the negative consequences that can result from negative thoughts, words, and actions. Negative karma can be resolved through positive thoughts, words, and actions, and can be a powerful motivator for individuals to live a more positive and virtuous life.

how negative karma can be resolved through positive actions can be seen in the life of the Dalai Lama. The Dalai Lama is the spiritual leader of Tibetan Buddhism and is known for his compassionate and selfless actions. Despite facing numerous challenges and difficulties in his life, including exile from his native Tibet, the Dalai Lama has maintained a positive outlook and has devoted his life to serving others.

Through his selfless actions and compassionate leadership, the Dalai Lama has created positive karma and resolved any negative karma from his past. He has dedicated his life to promoting peace, compassion, and understanding, and has inspired millions of people around the world to live a more virtuous life.

The Dalai Lama's life serves as a powerful example of how negative karma can be resolved through positive thoughts, words, and actions. He has shown that it is possible to overcome adversity and create a positive impact on the world through selfless service and compassion.

The life of the Dalai Lama is a real-life example of how negative karma can be resolved through positive actions. By living a virtuous life and devoting himself to serving others, the Dalai Lama has created positive karma and inspired millions of people around the world to live a more positive and meaningful life.

Recognizing the causes of negative Karma

In Hindu mythology, there are many examples of negative Karma being caused by various actions, thoughts, and intentions. One such example is from the epic, "Mahabharata."

The character Duryodhana, one of the hundred Kauravas, caused immense suffering and violence through his actions and intentions. He was driven by jealousy, greed, and a desire for power. This resulted in negative Karma for him and his family, ultimately leading to their downfall in the great battle of Kurukshetra.

An analogy to describe this could be: "Negative Karma is like a seed that is sown, and its fruit is reaped in due time. Just as a farmer carefully chooses the seeds they plant in their field, our thoughts, words, and actions determine the kind of Karma we create and its consequences."

In this example, we can see that the causes of negative Karma can stem from negative thoughts and intentions, such as jealousy, greed, and a desire for power. Understanding the causes of negative Karma is crucial for recognizing and breaking patterns of negative behavior and creating positive change in our lives.

One example of a spiritual leader who emphasizes the causes of negative Karma is Sri Sri Ravi Shankar, the founder of the Art of Living Foundation. He teaches that negative emotions such as anger, hatred, and resentment create negative Karma, while positive emotions such as love, kindness, and compassion create positive Karma.

Sri Sri Ravi Shankar often uses the analogy of a seed to explain the concept of Karma. He says, "Just as a seed needs the right conditions to grow, our thoughts, words, and actions need the right conditions to create positive or negative Karma. If we plant the seed of love, kindness, and compassion, it will grow into a tree of positive Karma that will bear fruit for us and those around us."

This analogy helps to understand that our thoughts, words, and actions are like seeds that we are constantly planting in our lives, and they will grow and bear fruit in due time. Recognizing the causes of negative Karma, and making conscious efforts to cultivate positive thoughts, words, and actions, can help us create positive Karma and bring happiness and peace into our lives.

Overcoming the effects of negative Karma

Overcoming the effects of negative Karma involves developing an understanding of the causes of negative Karma, and making conscious efforts to change negative patterns of behavior and thoughts. Here are a few ways to overcome the effects of negative Karma:

1. Self-reflection: Take time to reflect on your thoughts, words, and actions. Look for patterns of negative behavior and thoughts and acknowledge their impact on your life.
2. Cultivate positive emotions: Focus on cultivating positive emotions such as love, kindness, and compassion. Engage in activities that bring joy and positivity into your life.
3. Practice selflessness: Engage in selfless acts of kindness, service, and generosity. This can help to counteract the effects of negative Karma.
4. Forgiveness: Forgiving others and ourselves is essential in overcoming the effects of negative Karma. Holding onto anger, hatred, and resentment creates negative Karma, while forgiveness allows us to let go of these negative emotions and create positive Karma.
5. Mindfulness and meditation: Mindfulness and meditation can help to calm the mind and bring awareness to our thoughts and emotions. This can help to break negative patterns of behavior and thoughts, and create positive Karma.

By following these steps and making conscious efforts to change negative patterns of behavior and thoughts, we can overcome the effects of negative Karma and create positive Karma that will bring happiness and peace into our lives.

Transforming negative Karma

Transforming negative Karma into positive Karma involves recognizing and acknowledging negative patterns of behavior and thoughts, and making conscious efforts to change them. Here are a few steps to help transform negative Karma into positive Karma:

1. Awareness: The first step in transforming negative Karma is to become aware of it. Self-reflection and mindfulness can help to bring awareness to negative patterns of behavior and thoughts.
2. Acceptance: Acceptance is key in transforming negative Karma. Acknowledge your negative Karma, and be willing to work towards changing it.
3. Change negative behavior and thoughts: Once you are aware of your negative Karma, make an effort to change negative patterns of behavior and thoughts. Cultivate positive emotions, practice selflessness, and engage in activities that bring joy and positivity into your life.
4. Practice positive actions: Engage in positive actions, such as volunteering, helping others, and engaging in acts of kindness and compassion. These positive actions create positive Karma and help to counteract negative Karma.
5. Meditation and mindfulness: Meditation and mindfulness can help to calm the mind and bring awareness to our thoughts and emotions. This can help to break negative patterns of behavior and thoughts, and create positive Karma.

By following these steps and making conscious efforts to change negative patterns of behavior and thoughts, we can transform negative Karma into positive Karma and create a happier, more fulfilling life.

The role of self-reflection in reducing negative Karma

Self-reflection plays a crucial role in reducing negative Karma. By reflecting on one's actions and thoughts, individuals can gain a better understanding of their negative patterns and work towards changing them. Here are a few examples from the Dharmashastras on the importance of self-reflection in reducing negative Karma:

1. "One who knows the law should examine his own actions day and night." - Apastamba Dharmasutra
2. "A man who is always mindful of his own faults, and is constantly searching for ways to improve himself, will soon become free from all sins." - Manu Smriti
3. "The man who is self-controlled, who is tranquil, who has subdued his senses, and who is engaged in meditation and self-reflection, attains peace." - Bhagavad Gita
4. "The man who is introspective, who constantly reflects on his own actions, and who strives to do good, will soon attain the highest state of bliss." - Yajur Veda

These examples from the Dharmashastras emphasize the importance of self-reflection in reducing negative Karma. By reflecting on one's actions and thoughts, individuals can gain a deeper understanding of their negative patterns, make conscious efforts to change them, and create positive Karma.

The story of Ramayana is full of examples of the role of self-reflection in reducing negative Karma. Here are a few examples:

1. Rama's self-reflection during his exile in the forest: Rama, after being exiled from his kingdom, reflects on his actions and vows

to live a life of virtue and righteousness. This self-reflection leads him to attain spiritual enlightenment and become an embodiment of dharma.

2. Hanuman's self-reflection before meeting Sita: Hanuman, before meeting Sita, reflects on his actions and decides to control his passions and anger. This self-reflection leads him to become a model of devotion and courage.

3. Ravana's self-reflection before his defeat: Ravana, before his defeat, reflects on his actions and realizes that his pride and ego were the root cause of his downfall. This self-reflection, however, comes too late to change his fate.

These examples from the Ramayana highlight the importance of self-reflection in reducing negative Karma. By reflecting on one's actions and thoughts, individuals can gain a deeper understanding of their negative patterns and make conscious efforts to change them, thus transforming negative Karma into positive Karma.

CHAPTER FIVE

Practicing Positive Karma

In the practice of Positive Karma, individuals strive to cultivate virtuous thoughts, words, and actions that lead to a positive impact on themselves and others. This can be accomplished through various spiritual practices such as meditation, self-reflection, and acts of kindness and compassion.

One example of Positive Karma in action can be seen in the life of Mahatma Gandhi. Gandhi believed in the principle of Ahimsa, or non-violence, and strived to live a life of compassion and kindness. He used this philosophy to lead India's independence movement against British rule through peaceful means. By consistently choosing to act in a positive and non-violent manner, Gandhi was able to positively impact not only himself but also those around him and ultimately change the course of history.

Another example can be seen in the teachings of the Dalai Lama, who encourages individuals to practice altruism and compassion for the benefit of others. By focusing on the well-being of others and spreading positive energy, individuals can cultivate positive Karma that leads to happiness and inner peace.

In the practice of Positive Karma, it is important to remember that the effects of one's actions may not always be immediate, but the accumulation of positive actions over time will result in a positive impact on both the self and others.

The benefits of positive Karma

The benefits of Positive Karma are both immediate and long-term, affecting individuals on both a personal and collective level.

On a personal level, practicing Positive Karma can lead to increased feelings of happiness, inner peace, and contentment. This is because positive actions generate positive energy and thoughts, which in turn have a positive impact on an individual's overall well-being. Positive Karma also strengthens one's character, helping individuals develop qualities such as empathy, kindness, and compassion, which are essential for personal growth and fulfillment.

On a collective level, Positive Karma has the power to create a ripple effect of positivity, spreading kindness and compassion throughout communities and beyond. When individuals choose to act positively, they set an example for others to follow, creating a chain reaction of positive energy that can impact entire communities and even the world.

Additionally, Positive Karma has the potential to bring about transformative change on a global scale. By consistently choosing to act in a positive and compassionate manner, individuals can contribute to the creation of a more harmonious and equitable world.

the practice of Positive Karma not only benefits the individual, but also has the power to create a positive impact on the world. By consistently making positive choices, individuals can cultivate a life filled with happiness, inner peace, and a sense of purpose.

The cultivation of positive thoughts, words, and actions is an essential aspect of positive Karma. It is believed that one's thoughts, words, and actions are all interconnected, and that a change in one can have a profound impact on the other two. This idea is reflected in the teachings of the Upanishads, which are ancient Hindu scriptures that are considered to be the foundation of Hindu philosophy.

One of the key teachings of the Upanishads is that every thought, word, and action generates energy and creates an imprint on the universe. If these imprints are positive, they can bring happiness and prosperity to the individual, while negative imprints can lead to suffering and misfortune.

The Upanishads also emphasize the importance of mindfulness and self-awareness in cultivating positive thoughts, words, and actions. By being mindful of our thoughts, words, and actions, we can develop the ability to choose our responses in a way that supports positive Karma.

One example of how this principle can be applied in real life is through the practice of meditation. By regularly meditating, an individual can gain greater control over their thoughts and emotions, which can lead to more positive thoughts, words, and actions. Through consistent practice, this can become a habit that helps to cultivate positive Karma over time.

the Upanishads offer valuable insights into the relationship between positive thoughts, words, and actions and positive Karma. By incorporating these teachings into our lives, we can cultivate positive Karma and reap the benefits of a more fulfilling and harmonious life.

The cultivation of positive thoughts,

The cultivation of positive thoughts, words, and actions is an essential aspect of positive Karma. It is believed that one's thoughts, words, and actions are all interconnected, and that a change in one can have a profound impact on the other two. This idea is reflected in the teachings of the Upanishads, which are ancient Hindu scriptures that are considered to be the foundation of Hindu philosophy.

One of the key teachings of the Upanishads is that every thought, word, and action generates energy and creates an imprint on the universe. If these imprints are positive, they can bring happiness and prosperity to the individual, while negative imprints can lead to suffering and misfortune.

The Upanishads also emphasize the importance of mindfulness and self-awareness in cultivating positive thoughts, words, and actions. By being mindful of our thoughts, words, and actions, we can develop the ability to choose our responses in a way that supports positive Karma.

One example of how this principle can be applied in real life is through the practice of meditation. By regularly meditating, an individual can gain greater control over their thoughts and emotions, which can lead to more positive thoughts, words, and actions. Through consistent practice, this can become a habit that helps to cultivate positive Karma over time.

the Upanishads offer valuable insights into the relationship between positive thoughts, words, and actions and positive Karma. By incorporating these teachings into our lives, we can cultivate positive Karma and reap the benefits of a more fulfilling and harmonious life.

Practicing generosity, compassion, and kindness

The practice of generosity, compassion, and kindness plays a crucial role in shaping positive karma. A great example of these values can be seen in the character of Lord Rama from the Hindu epic, Ramayana. Rama, who is regarded as the seventh avatar of Lord Vishnu, was known for his unwavering devotion to righteousness and compassion towards all living beings. Throughout the Ramayana, Rama demonstrated the practice of generosity by constantly helping those in need, compassion by showing empathy towards all creatures, and kindness by always treating others with dignity and respect.

One such instance is when Rama rescued Sita, his wife, who had been kidnapped by the demon king, Ravana. Despite being offered help from various powerful beings, Rama chose to undertake the journey alone to rescue Sita. This act of bravery and compassion towards his wife showcases Rama's unwavering commitment to positive karma.

Another instance is when Rama, along with his brother, Lakshmana, encountered the demoness, Surpanakha. Despite her attempts to harm them, Rama chose to spare her life and offered her advice on how to lead a virtuous life, displaying his compassion and kindness towards all living beings, regardless of their actions.

Through his actions and character, Lord Rama serves as an excellent example of how one can cultivate positive thoughts, words, and actions, thereby shaping their karma in a positive direction.

Krishna, one of the most revered deities in Hinduism, is a great example of the practice of generosity, compassion, and kindness. Throughout the Hindu epic "Mahabharata," Krishna demonstrates these qualities in numerous ways. For example, Krishna is known for his unwavering devotion to justice and his unending compassion for all living beings. He constantly gives of himself, providing guidance, support, and protection to those who seek it.

One famous example of Krishna's generosity is when he lifted the Govardhan Hill to protect the villagers of Vrindavan from a raging storm. Despite the immense effort required, Krishna did not hesitate to help those in need. Additionally, Krishna showed great compassion for the fallen warrior Arjuna, offering him counsel and support during the great battle of Kurukshetra.

Krishna also embodies the qualities of kindness and compassion. He never acted with ill will or malice, and always sought to help others, even if it meant putting himself in harm's way. These qualities have made Krishna a revered figure in Hinduism and a shining example of the power of positive Karma. By following his example, one can cultivate the qualities of generosity, compassion, and kindness, and thereby improve their own karma and spiritual evolution.

Engaging in selfless acts for the greater good

Selfless acts have been a common theme throughout many spiritual leaders' lives and teachings. For example, Mahatma Gandhi was known for his philosophy of nonviolence and selfless service to others. He believed that every act of kindness, no matter how small, can bring positive change to the world. He lived this belief by dedicating his life to the betterment of India and its people, working tirelessly to promote peace, justice, and equality.

The Mahabharata War provides several examples of selfless acts for the greater good. One such instance is that of Arjuna, who initially hesitates to fight in the war, but eventually realizes the importance of fulfilling his duty to protect dharma and engage in the fight. Another example is that of Karna, who, despite his allegiance to the Kauravas, offers his services and ultimately sacrifices his life for the greater good of the war. These examples demonstrate the importance of engaging in selfless acts, even in times of conflict, for the greater good of society and the larger moral and ethical principles it upholds.

CHAPTER SIX

Karma in Relationships

1. Karma plays an important role in shaping our relationships, as it shapes the way we interact with others and can impact the way they treat us in return. The puranas contain numerous examples of how Karma affects relationships.

2. For instance, in the Ramayana, the relationship between Rama and his wife Sita is impacted by Karma. Sita is abducted by the demon king Ravana and Rama goes to great lengths to rescue her, demonstrating his unwavering devotion and love. This selfless act of Rama is a reflection of his positive Karma, and it ultimately leads to the reunion of the couple and their happy life together.

3. Similarly, in the Mahabharata, the relationships between the characters are shaped by their Karma. The Pandavas, who are known for their good Karma, are always helped by divine forces and are able to overcome obstacles in their journey. On the other hand, the Kauravas, who have accumulated negative Karma through their actions, face numerous challenges and ultimately meet their downfall.

4. These examples demonstrate the power of Karma in shaping relationships, and highlight the importance of cultivating positive thoughts, words, and actions to improve our relationships and the experiences we have with others.

5. Karma plays a significant role in shaping our relationships, both personal and professional. In Hindu mythology, the Puranas

often showcase the impact of Karma on relationships through various characters and their actions. For example, in the Ramayana, Lord Rama's actions and decision-making were guided by his sense of dharma, or duty, and his actions ultimately determined the outcome of his relationships with his wife Sita, brother Lakshmana, and friends.

6. In real life, the impact of Karma on relationships can be seen in how our thoughts, words, and actions shape the way others perceive us and interact with us. If we act with kindness and compassion, we are likely to attract positive relationships and experiences, while negative actions and behaviors can lead to conflicts and strained relationships.

7. For instance, consider a person who constantly speaks negatively about others and spreads rumors. Such behavior may cause others to distance themselves and eventually, the individual may find themselves isolated and with few close relationships. On the other hand, someone who consistently treats others with kindness and respect is more likely to build strong and positive relationships.

8. Thus, it is essential to be mindful of our actions and the impact they may have on our relationships and strive to cultivate positive Karma through our thoughts, words, and actions.

Building positive Karma in relationships

In the story of King Janaka and Sage Yajnavalkya from the Hindu scripture, Brihadaranyaka Upanishad. King Janaka was a just and wise ruler who was deeply committed to his own spiritual growth. One day, he invited Sage Yajnavalkya to his court to participate in a philosophical discussion. During the discussion, King Janaka asked the sage to explain the nature of the self.

Sage Yajnavalkya gave a profound response that not only enlightened King Janaka, but also demonstrated the importance of building positive Karma in relationships. He said, "The self is not the body, nor the senses, nor the mind. The self is the eternal witness, the source of consciousness, and the foundation of all experiences."

King Janaka was deeply moved by the sage's teachings and felt a strong connection to him. He realized that his relationship with Sage Yajnavalkya was based on mutual respect, love, and a shared pursuit of spiritual growth. King Janaka was grateful for the sage's wisdom and decided to honor him by offering him a gift. He gave him one of his most valuable possessions, a herd of cows, as a symbol of his respect and gratitude.

In this story, King Janaka demonstrated the power of building positive Karma in relationships. He recognized the importance of nurturing his relationship with Sage Yajnavalkya and showed his appreciation through acts of generosity and kindness. By doing so, King Janaka not only enriched his own life, but also created a foundation of positive Karma that would benefit him in future lives.

This story serves as a reminder that our relationships with others have a profound impact on our spiritual growth and the quality of our lives. By building positive Karma in our relationships, we create a positive foundation for our future and contribute to the well-being of those around us.

The role of forgiveness and understanding in transforming Karma

In dealing with negative Karma in relationships, it is important to understand that the way we interact with others has a significant impact on the quality of our relationships. Negative Karma, or the accumulation of negative actions, thoughts, and emotions, can lead to conflict, tension, and disharmony in our relationships. However, with conscious effort and self-reflection, it is possible to turn this negative Karma into positive Karma, and create harmonious and fulfilling relationships.

One approach to dealing with negative Karma in relationships is to cultivate a sense of compassion and understanding towards others. This involves recognizing that everyone has their own challenges and struggles, and making an effort to see things from their perspective. By doing so, we can reduce the judgment and criticism that can lead to negative Karma, and instead cultivate a sense of empathy and connection with those around us.

Another approach is to engage in selfless acts for the greater good of the relationship. This could involve making sacrifices for the benefit of the other person, or taking steps to resolve conflicts and heal any wounds. By acting selflessly, we create positive Karma that can help to heal and strengthen our relationships, and reduce the impact of negative Karma.

Finally, it is important to regularly reflect on our thoughts, words, and actions, and assess their impact on our relationships. By doing so, we can identify and address any negative patterns that may be causing harm, and cultivate a more positive and harmonious way of interacting with others.

CHAPTER SEVEN

Karma and the Environment

The impact of our actions on the environment is a significant aspect of Karma as it highlights the consequences of our choices and actions. The Hindu philosophy teaches us that everything in the universe is interconnected, and our actions have a ripple effect on the environment and the world around us.

For example, in Hindu mythology, the story of Lord Vishnu's second avatar, Kurma, serves as an analogy for the impact of human actions on the environment. According to the story, Lord Vishnu took the form of a turtle to support the mount Mandara, which was being used as a churning rod to produce the elixir of life. The story symbolizes how human actions can impact the environment, as in this case, the mount Mandara represents the earth, and the churning symbolizes human activities that disturb the balance of nature.

Similarly, in real life, human activities such as deforestation, pollution, and overconsumption of resources can harm the environment and create negative consequences for future generations. Hence, it's crucial to understand the impact of our actions on the environment and make conscious choices to build positive Karma.

The role of Karma in environmental conservation In Hindu philosophy, Karma is not just limited to the individual level but also extends to the collective level, including the environment. The environment and all its inhabitants are interdependent and connected, and any harm to one part of the environment will have a ripple effect on all other parts. The same holds true for positive actions towards the environment. By living sustainably and promoting eco-friendliness, individuals can help conserve the environment and reduce negative Karma, leading to a better world for all.

One example of this is the Hindu spiritual leader, Sadhguru Jaggi Vasudev. He emphasizes the importance of being mindful of one's actions and their impact on the environment. Sadhguru encourages individuals to adopt sustainable living practices, such as reducing their carbon footprint, conserving water, and using renewable energy sources. He also encourages people to take a step further and actively participate in environmental conservation efforts, such as planting trees, cleaning up beaches and forests, and reducing waste.

By taking these actions, individuals can reduce their negative impact on the environment and cultivate positive Karma. This, in turn, can lead to a harmonious relationship between humans and the environment, preserving it for future generations.

The benefits of creating positive Karma for the environment

Positive Karma can have a profound impact on the environment and the world we live in. By making conscious choices to live sustainably, protect natural resources, and promote eco-friendliness, individuals can create positive Karma and help ensure a healthy planet for future generations. Here are some of the key benefits of creating positive Karma for the environment:

1. Preservation of Natural Resources: By living sustainably, we can help preserve valuable natural resources, such as clean water, fresh air, and fertile soil, for future generations.
2. Reduction of Pollution: Simple actions such as reducing energy consumption, using public transportation, and recycling can help reduce pollution and prevent further damage to the environment.
3. Protection of Endangered Species: By supporting eco-friendly initiatives, we can help protect endangered species and preserve biodiversity.
4. Improved Health: A healthy environment is essential for our well-being and the health of future generations. By creating positive Karma for the environment, we can help promote clean air and water, which can lead to improved health outcomes.
5. Increased Happiness: Studies have shown that individuals who engage in eco-friendly activities and live sustainably are happier and have a greater sense of purpose. By creating positive Karma for the environment, individuals can experience these benefits and contribute to a happier and healthier world.

By creating positive Karma for the environment, individuals can help preserve valuable natural resources, reduce pollution, protect endangered species, and promote a healthy and happy world for future generations.

Karma and the Environment

The journey to overcome the challenges of Karma is not an easy one, but it is a necessary one to achieve personal growth and inner peace. One of the biggest challenges is to recognize negative patterns and tendencies in our thoughts and actions. Self-reflection, mindfulness, and introspection can help us identify these patterns and work towards transforming them.

Another challenge is to cultivate positive habits and make them a part of our daily routine. This requires discipline and effort, but the benefits of creating positive Karma are worth the effort.

It is also important to cultivate a positive and supportive environment, surrounded by people who encourage and motivate us to make positive changes in our lives. Joining a community of like-minded individuals or seeking guidance from a spiritual leader can help us in our journey.

Ultimately, the key to overcoming the challenges of Karma is to have a clear intention and purpose, and to believe in our ability to make positive changes in our lives. With patience, persistence, and determination, we can overcome any obstacle and create a life filled with positive Karma.

Understanding the challenges of Karma

In the journey of life, we often encounter many challenges that may hinder our progress and prevent us from reaching our full potential. Similarly, in the journey of Karma, there are several challenges that may obstruct our efforts to create positive Karma and overcome negative Karma. These challenges can come in various forms such as negative thoughts, destructive behaviors, lack of self-reflection, and limited awareness about the laws of Karma.

It is essential to understand these challenges and take proactive measures to overcome them. This can be achieved through self-awareness, self-reflection, and a commitment to engage in positive actions that can create positive Karma and transform negative Karma into positive Karma. By overcoming the challenges of Karma, we can lead a more fulfilling and meaningful life, attain inner peace and happiness, and make a positive impact on the world around us.

Overcoming obstacles to positive Karma

Continuing from the previous topic, understanding the challenges of Karma, one significant aspect of overcoming obstacles to positive Karma is recognizing that change requires effort and perseverance. The journey towards positive Karma is not always smooth, and one may face obstacles along the way. However, with determination and the right attitude, one can overcome these challenges and continue on the path towards positive Karma.

One of the biggest obstacles is our own mind and thoughts. Our thoughts and beliefs can limit us, and negative self-talk can hold us back from making positive changes. To overcome this obstacle, it is essential to cultivate a positive mindset, engage in regular self-reflection, and practice self-compassion.

Another obstacle to positive Karma is our environment and the people around us. Society and the world at large can have a significant impact on our behavior and thoughts. To overcome this obstacle, it is crucial to surround oneself with positive and supportive individuals who encourage growth and positivity.

Lastly, habits and routines can be a significant obstacle to positive Karma. Breaking old habits and adopting new ones takes time, effort, and discipline. However, with practice and perseverance, one can develop new habits and routines that align with the pursuit of positive Karma.

The journey towards positive Karma may have its challenges, but with the right mindset and approach, one can overcome obstacles and continue on the path towards a fulfilling and meaningful life.

In order to overcome obstacles to positive Karma, determination and perseverance are crucial qualities to possess. These qualities help individuals stay focused on their goals and continue to make efforts towards creating positive Karma, even when faced with challenges.

One example of determination and perseverance in overcoming Karma can be found in the Hindu mythology of Lord Rama. Rama was faced with numerous challenges, including the loss of his wife Sita, during his journey to become the king of Ayodhya. However, despite these difficulties, Rama remained steadfast in his efforts to maintain his righteousness and perform good deeds. This determination and perseverance allowed Rama to overcome the obstacles in his path and create positive Karma for himself.

Another example can be found in the life of Mahatma Gandhi, who used his determination and perseverance to lead the Indian independence movement against British rule. Despite facing numerous challenges, including imprisonment and acts of violence against him, Gandhi never wavered in his commitment to non-violent resistance and creating positive Karma through his actions.

determination and perseverance play a crucial role in overcoming obstacles to creating positive Karma. By staying focused on one's goals and continuing to make efforts towards positive actions, individuals can overcome challenges and create a positive impact in the world.

The benefits of overcoming challenges to positive Karma

Overcoming the challenges to positive Karma can bring many benefits to our lives. Firstly, it can help us to cultivate a stronger sense of self-awareness and responsibility. When we understand the consequences of our actions, we become more mindful of the choices we make and the impact they have on ourselves and others.

Secondly, overcoming the challenges of Karma can also lead to greater inner peace and happiness. By reducing negative Karma and increasing positive Karma, we can reduce our suffering and experience more positive emotions and experiences.

Finally, overcoming the challenges of Karma can also lead to spiritual growth and liberation. By working to create positive Karma, we can gradually purify our minds and become more aligned with our true nature, freeing ourselves from the cycle of reincarnation and experiencing ultimate liberation.

In the Mahabharata, we can see examples of overcoming challenges to positive Karma in the characters of Bhishma, Arjuna, and Yudhishthira. Bhishma, known for his unwavering determination and loyalty, serves as an example of perseverance in the face of obstacles. Arjuna, with his deep understanding of Dharma and unwavering commitment to righteousness, demonstrates the importance of following one's conscience and standing up for what is right. Finally, Yudhishthira, with his wisdom and fairness, embodies the importance of living in alignment with one's values and making decisions that are both just and compassionate. These characters can serve as inspiration and guidance for us as we work to overcome the challenges to positive Karma in our own lives.

1. The determination of Arjuna: In the epic of Mahabharata, Arjuna faced many challenges in his journey towards positive Karma. Despite facing obstacles, he persevered and remained steadfast in his resolve to do the right thing. This determination is a valuable lesson for today's society as it highlights the importance of staying focused and committed to creating positive Karma, even in the face of adversity.

2. The perseverance of Bhishma: Bhishma is another example from the Mahabharata who demonstrated the power of perseverance. Despite facing numerous challenges and setbacks, he remained committed to his principles and never wavered in his quest for positive Karma. In modern society, this lesson can be applied to individuals who are seeking to create positive change, as it highlights the importance of staying the course and never giving up, even in the face of difficulty.

3. The resilience of Yudhishthira: Yudhishthira, the eldest of the Pandavas, faced many challenges in his quest for positive Karma. However, despite these obstacles, he remained resilient and continued to strive towards his goal. This example is a valuable lesson for today's society, as it highlights the importance of resilience and perseverance in overcoming the challenges of Karma. Whether it be in personal or professional life, maintaining a resilient and determined mindset can help individuals overcome obstacles and achieve their goals.

CHAPTER NINE

Karma's Life 21 Tips

Karma's Life 21 Tips

1. Cultivate mindfulness and self-awareness, and reflect on the impact of your thoughts, words, and actions.
2. Practice compassion and empathy, and strive to act with kindness and generosity towards others.
3. Take responsibility for your actions and strive to make amends for past mistakes.
4. Be mindful of your thoughts and feelings, and seek to cultivate positive emotions such as gratitude and joy.
5. Make a conscious effort to live a virtuous life, and strive to avoid negative actions that create negative karma.
6. Practice forgiveness, both for yourself and others, and seek to release negative emotions such as anger and resentment.

7. Cultivate positive relationships with others, and strive to build strong and meaningful connections with family, friends, and community.

8. Give back to your community and contribute to the greater good, whether through volunteering, donating to charity, or simply being kind to others.

9. Develop a daily spiritual practice, such as meditation, prayer, or mindfulness, that helps you connect with your inner self and the world around you.

10. Seek out wisdom and knowledge, and strive to expand your understanding of the world and the workings of karma.

11. Treat all beings with respect, whether they be human, animal, or plant, and seek to minimize harm to all forms of life.

12. Be mindful of your consumption habits, and seek to minimize waste and reduce your impact on the environment.

13. Strive to live a balanced life, with a focus on physical, mental, and spiritual well-being.

14. Seek out opportunities to help others, whether through volunteering, donating to charity, or simply being there for someone in need.

15. Practice gratitude and appreciate the good things in your life, no matter how small or seemingly insignificant they may seem.

16. Cultivate a positive outlook, and seek to focus on the good in life, even in the face of adversity.

17. Seek out positive role models and surround yourself with people who inspire and uplift you.

18. Strive to be honest and truthful in your interactions with others, and avoid engaging in harmful or deceitful behavior.

19. Be mindful of your own limitations, and seek to grow and develop as a person, both intellectually and spiritually.

20. Embrace change, and see it as an opportunity for growth and transformation.

Remember that the journey of creating positive karma is a lifelong process, and seek to live each day with purpose and intention.

The conclusion of the book "Karma's Signature" is the summation of the journey through the philosophies, principles and practical aspects of Karma. Karma, a fundamental concept in many ancient wisdom traditions, teaches us that our thoughts, words, and actions have consequences that shape our present and future. To truly understand and live by the principles of Karma, it's crucial to embody its teachings in our daily lives.

Here are 9 tips to deepen your understanding of Karma:

1. Reflect on your actions: Take time to reflect on the choices you make and how they impact yourself and others.
2. Practice mindfulness: By being present in each moment, you can make conscious decisions that align with your values and principles.
3. Cultivate compassion: Empathy and kindness towards others will bring more positivity into your life and help you understand the interconnectedness of all beings.
4. Act with intention: Make conscious choices, and act with intention and purpose, knowing that each decision will have a ripple effect.
5. Embrace non-attachment: Letting go of material desires and attachments can bring peace and liberation to your life.
6. Seek wisdom: Learn from the teachings of spiritual leaders and ancient wisdom traditions to deepen your understanding of Karma.
7. Practice gratitude: Expressing gratitude for what you have and the positive experiences in your life can bring a deeper appreciation and connection to the world.

8. Let go of judgment: Avoid judging yourself or others and cultivate a non-judgmental attitude, which can help you see the world with a more compassionate lens.

9. Live with purpose: By living a life with purpose and intention, you can fulfill your potential and make a positive impact in the world.

By incorporating these tips into your life, you can deepen your understanding of Karma and live a more fulfilling, meaningful life.

CHAPTER TEN

Conclusion

The concept of Karma has been a central teaching in Hinduism and Buddhism, and it holds that our actions and thoughts have consequences, both in this life and future lives. The Upanishads, ancient Hindu scriptures, illustrate the significance of Karma in our lives through various allegories and stories.

One such story is the allegory of the two birds. In this allegory, the human soul is compared to two birds, one bird sitting on a tree and the other bird flying freely. The bird that is sitting on the tree represents the material self, and the bird that is flying represents the spiritual self. The material self is bound by the laws of Karma and is constantly in the cycle of birth and death, while the spiritual self is free and eternal. The story suggests that it is our actions and thoughts that determine the fate of the material self, and that we have the power to move towards liberation by performing good deeds and purifying our minds.

This allegory highlights the significance of Karma in our lives by emphasizing that our actions and thoughts determine our fate. It reminds us that we have the power to change our destiny by performing good deeds and cultivating positive thoughts and actions. The Upanishads emphasize that the path of righteousness, or Dharma, is the way to liberation and that by following this path, we can overcome the laws of Karma and attain a state of peace and happiness.

In today's context, this analogy can be interpreted as a reminder to live a life of mindfulness, where our actions are guided by our values and beliefs. We must strive to make ethical and sustainable choices in our daily lives, and be mindful of the impact that our actions have on others and the environment. By doing so, we can create positive Karma and live a fulfilling and meaningful life.

The impact of Karma on personal growth and happiness

In Hindu philosophy, Karma is believed to have a significant impact on a person's growth and happiness. According to the teachings of Upanishads, the choices we make in our lives determine the kind of Karma we create, which in turn affects our future experiences. If we perform actions that are good, virtuous, and moral, we create positive Karma, which leads to growth, happiness, and contentment. On the other hand, if we engage in actions that are harmful, unethical, or negative, we create negative Karma, which brings about suffering, misery, and unhappiness.

An example from the Upanishads to illustrate this concept is the story of King Janaka. King Janaka was a just and fair ruler who always acted with compassion and wisdom. As a result, he created positive Karma, which brought about happiness, peace, and prosperity in his kingdom. Despite his wealth and power, King Janaka never let his ego get the best of him, and he always lived a life of humility and selflessness. This earned him a place among the greatest of Hindu spiritual leaders, and his story continues to inspire people to this day.

The analogy of King Janaka's life to our own lives is that by making wise, compassionate, and virtuous choices, we can create positive Karma and lead a life of happiness, peace, and prosperity. On the other hand, by engaging in negative and unethical behaviors, we create negative Karma, which leads to suffering, misery, and unhappiness. The impact of Karma on personal growth and happiness is a reminder to us all that our actions have consequences, and that we must be mindful of the choices we make in life.

Karma is a central concept in Hinduism and many other Eastern spiritual traditions, and it is closely linked to the idea that our actions have consequences, both in this life and in future lives. Understanding and practicing Karma is essential for personal growth and happiness because it helps us to align our thoughts, words, and actions with the greater good, and to cultivate positive qualities like generosity, compassion, and kindness.

Through practicing Karma, we can create positive energy that supports our own well-being and the well-being of others. By engaging in selfless acts and avoiding negative actions, we can also reduce the negative effects of past Karma and create a better future for ourselves and those around us.

One of the Upanishads, a Hindu scripture, states that "As a man acts, so does he become. As he becomes, so does he act." This statement highlights the cyclical nature of Karma and the importance of our actions in shaping our lives. Through understanding and practicing Karma, we can take control of our lives and create positive change in the world.

In conclusion, understanding and practicing Karma is a valuable path to personal growth and happiness, and is an essential aspect of many Eastern spiritual traditions. By embracing this philosophy and aligning our thoughts, words, and actions with the greater good, we can create a more harmonious and fulfilling life for ourselves and those around us.

Our Memories

Our Media Presence

Our Healing Classes

Our Energy Healing Classes

Our Energy Healing Classes

Our Energy Healing Classes

Our Memories

Our Feathers

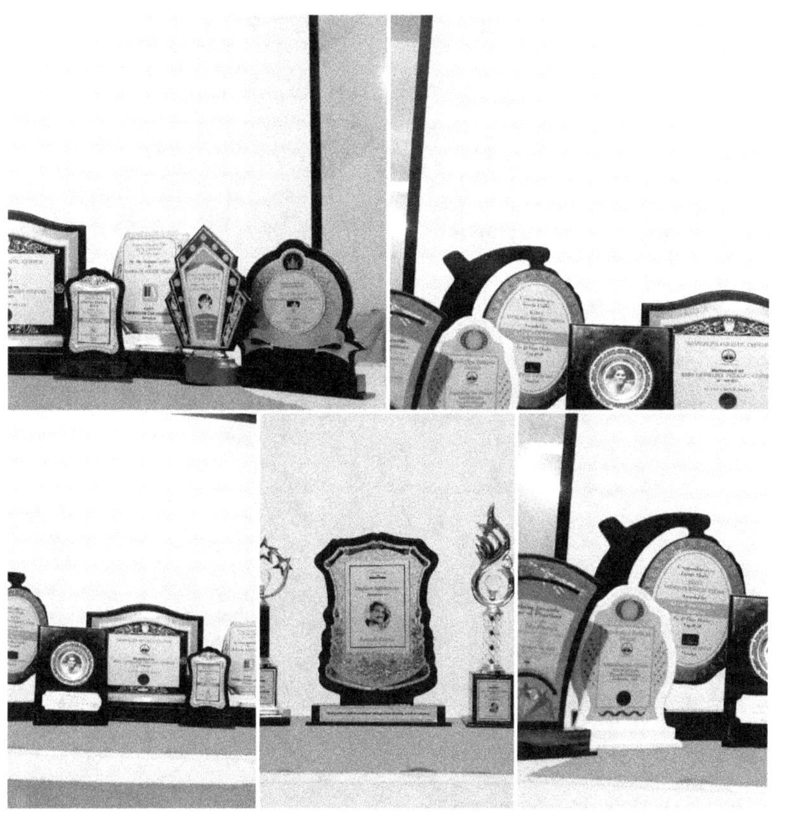

Enter Caption

How To Reach Us

Savikalpa Holistic Center

Youtube @Savikalpaholisticcenter
Facebook Savikalpa Holistic Center
Contact Number : 6364795551 / 9538735551

Our Other Books

Free 30 Mins Counselling Session